Contents

FOREWORD..3

CHAPTER 1. OUR HISTORY 7

CHAPTER 2. HOW DID WE GET WHERE WE ARE TODAY?..31

CHAPTER 3. WHAT ARE WE GONNA DO ABOUT IT?..63

CHAPTER 4. ONLY WAY TO SAVE AMERICA! 93

References 131

FOREWORD

I'm sure you're wondering who *States' Rights Citizen* is. Well, I decided not to use my real name because, number one, I don't want to take credit for the information I've included in this book. This information is out there available to us all if we would just take the time to do our own research, talk to people who are in the know, and put the pieces together, which I've done for you.

Number two, although you may not think that I have the credentials to be an expert on this subject, I believe that as an ordinary American citizen who cares about our country, and pays attention to what is going on, I have all the credentials necessary to speak on this subject, to warn you of things to come if we don't take action to stop what's coming to America.

I do work for a Fortune 500 company and have many years' experience writing technical books, and even taught writing at the college level, so in that regard, I have the credentials and know how to research and gather information to be able to write and publish a book, such as this one.

Also, I ask that you read this book and pass it on to others, who will pass it on to others, who may pass it on to someone who has the authority, like a state legislator or Governor, to do something about turning our country around – back to the America our founding fathers intended it to be. Once the America we all grew up with is gone, it will be gone forever!

Don't put all your faith in one man who has promised to make America great again. He can't do it without your help.

God Bless You and God Bless America!

This book is dedicated to all those whose eyes have yet to be opened about the truth!

Special thanks to my friends Emily and Kelly for helping with the editing of this book.

To join the States' Rights Now team or find out more about what you can do

to execute states' rights in your state, send email to: statesrightsb4gone@gmail.com

CHAPTER 1. OUR HISTORY

In America, there was a time when we were overtaxed, overburdened, under represented, and all individual dreams seemed to be regulated by a central power.

You may be thinking I'm talking about yesterday. I'm not. I'm talking about some two-hundred years ago, when our founding fathers (our forefathers) were in a situation where they were being ruled by an island and a controlling king far away. This king robbed them of the opportunities they came to this country to start, and to grow. *They* complained about taxation without representation.

That island was England, that King was King George III. Today, we find that this same island has been replaced by another island although this island is not surrounded by water, but it *is* an island nonetheless, called Washington D.C. Where water protected the shores of England, the island of Washington D.C. is protected by a *sea* of lobbyists, special interests, and money. The king has been replaced by a ruling class of elites who have taken the power away from the people.

We don't have the power anymore to control our own destiny. We the people - *don't.* It's been *taken* from us, and replaced by a ruling class disguised by a two-party system, designed of course, to entertain us, and make us believe that no matter which side of the political scale we fall on, that we have representation –

but we don't! They don't listen. They have no reason to listen. Consequently, we have lost our power over them to rule with fairness, as stipulated in our Constitution.

Now, our founding fathers, when faced with this situation, were forced to do something that most, of that day, did not want to do, and that was *revolution*. All they wanted was to be treated fairly. All they wanted was to be able to live the dream that they had come to this nation of abundance to live. They didn't come here to remain under the thumb and control of an evil king, a dictatorial king, that wanted to rob and plunder them for everything they worked so hard for and to bring out of the soil to grow.

Here we are today, no we don't have an evil king, but we have evil leaders and an evil government, just as evil as the king of old. We don't want to have to do what our forefathers did, which was to take up arms in a full revolt to win back our freedoms. You see, they never had it. They had to fight to get it. We've had it, but we've lost it.

Recently, we had an election. Most everyone that's reading this book knows the outcome. Donald Trump won. He beat Hillary Rodham Clinton in a race that was impossible. No one figured it would come out that way. But, the people rose up and he won. Unfortunately, many people believe that we had a great victory that day and now we are safe. Let me assure you, that day we *did* have a great victory. But, it was a victory in a battle, the *war* wages on.

The war I speak of is that of what we have given up. You see, what makes this such a horrible situation for us in America, is that no one took up arms against us and took it away from us, we gave it up of our own free will. You may be asking, what am I talking about? Well, let me give you a little history.

You see, once our founding fathers fought the Revolutionary War *and won*, they were left with a problem. Now that they were free of the king, what should they do? What kind of government would be ideal for us in America? They didn't know. They knew it wasn't a democracy. They were smart enough to know that a democracy, an honest and true democracy, never worked. Going all the way back through time, it *never* worked.[1] There had to be something else. Because with a democracy, all you had to do was eventually get enough people to go along with you, and then whatever that group wants, they would control the purse, and they'd get it. They knew that couldn't be. They knew also that there were regions in America where the population was greater than other parts of the country. In the populated areas, you'd put an unfair burden on the lesser populated regions. So, they came up with a new concept.

This new concept was called a *representative republic*, designed to balance things out, to make things fair geographically for everyone, taking into consideration the disproportionate population areas, the rich and the poor, no matter the race. From that day forward, we were a *representative republic.*

I heard this example once about what the difference is between a democracy (majority rules), which we are not, and a republic (rule of law). In this example, you have three animals, two are wolves and one is a sheep.

In a democracy, the sheep has no rights and becomes dinner. But, in a republic, governed by laws that treat everyone the same, the sheep is free and the wolves are just frustrated. If the wolves disregard the law and eat the sheep anyway, they are punished. That doesn't mean that the wolves won't try in every way possible to have the sheep for dinner, but if the people ensure that the rule of law is followed, the sheep will always be treated fairly.

The people must remain vigilant and ensure that those they elect to represent them are following the rule of law that the people put into place through them. If they don't, the wolves will take over. Today in America, the wolves have taken over Washington D.C., but they haven't yet taken over the states. Well, maybe some states, but not all states, at least not yet.

Our founding fathers wrote a Constitution. A Constitution that I believe was developed with divine intervention. After all, our founding fathers were all strong in their faith in God, the God of the Bible. In fact, much of our laws, even today, are based on Biblical law. Don't believe me? Go read the Bible, especially the Book of Deuteronomy. Why do you think our founders believed that only a natural born citizen could become president? Read Deuteronomy 17:15. Did you know that of all the nations in the world during Bible times, the Hebrews were the *only* people who treated their women with respect and honor, and even allowed them to own businesses and land? The *only* people who were commanded by God to treat their slaves with fairness, and even commanded them to let many go free after they fulfilled their obligation to their masters[2].

They didn't write 20,000 pages of laws for this land. They gave us our Constitution. Very simply written, very simply spoken. The amazing thing about our Constitution was the fact that they acknowledged that they didn't know what was right for the future. But, they did trust God and the laws that He set forth for mankind to live by in peace and harmony. So, they drafted a Constitution that ensured that the least of us, we the people, would be in charge of our destiny. That never again, would one person, or one controlling group, dictate for all people in this country the way things would be and how we would live.

Now, they gave us many amendments. But, the one we need

to call on today, is so critical for our time, and that is the Tenth Amendment. Now, some of you know what the Tenth Amendment is and what it's about. Probably the majority of you think you do, but you don't. Simply stated, the Tenth Amendment was our founding fathers' way of ensuring that the least of us, we the people, could control our own destiny. It was a way to prevent the eventuality of our central government in Washington D.C. getting control and ruling, much as it's doing today. They were smart enough to know from the day our nation was born that there would be people that would spend every moment of their life trying to become the power over this great nation. So, they gave us the Tenth Amendment as our defense for a time such as now.

The Tenth Amendment says that Washington D.C. (or the Federal government) has very limited powers. The power over the people should be entrusted to the States. We were meant to be a bottom-up government, not a top-down government. But, throughout the years what we have done, and I say all of us, what we have done is that we have seceded, given up the power of the state, in the interest of passing it on to the Federal government. We thought, we elected them, we're too busy, we don't want to mess with it, so let them handle it. Handle it they have. Every day we wake up and one more freedom we had yesterday is gone. We need to have that revolution our founding fathers had. But what is so significant about our modern revolution, is that we don't have to use bombs and bullets. All we need to do is stand up and claim back those powers that we have wrongly, over time, given to that island, we know now as Washington D.C.

During the battle of Trump vs Clinton, in that infamous battle, there was a slogan, *drain the swamp.* It was obvious during the campaign that the people in America, both liberal and conservative, were *tired* of the abuse and the control coming out of Washington, from both parties. So, they revolted in that battle and stood up and said *no more*. Again, one of the slogans that prevailed was *drain the swamp*. Meaning get *rid* of these people. Get rid of these people that go there and *stay* there. Get rid of these people that personally profit from selling our freedoms.

How do you drain the swamp? One suggestion was, we can put term limits on our members of Congress and the Senate. That'll never work. It would be a wonderful thing if it did, but it'll never work, because that means we'd have to go to our Congress and to our Senate and get them to regulate themselves and limit themselves to two terms or whatever limits we want to put on them. They'll *never* vote themselves to limit their number of terms, there's too much money, too much power at stake. It just won't work.

So how do you drain the swamp? Well, you can't win elections without money. Remember, I told you that the island of Washington D.C. is surrounded by lobbyists and money. One of the ways you drain the swamp is you take the Politicians in Washington and you strip them of the power to sell our future and our lives. That way, the lobbyists have nothing to buy. Sounds good, but how do you do it? States' rights!

All roads to freedom lead to states' rights. As you will learn, as we move beyond our history and look towards the future, the simple procedure of re-implementing that which is ours to have and to use will win a war that we're in right now. So, be careful all of you. Don't win a battle then relax. The war is not over, it's just begun.

CHAPTER 2. HOW DID WE GET WHERE WE ARE TODAY?

In this chapter, I will be bouncing around in time. Some things we'll go way back, some things we'll go not so far back. But, please bear with me, because how we got where we are today, is the roadmap to how we get out and get back to where we're supposed to be.

Now, everybody says it started in 1776, our Revolutionary War. Well, part of it did. During that period, the people in America, felt the sting of being overtaxed and overburdened by the King of England. This taxation, they thought was very unfair, especially when you considered that they had no say in it. In the early colonies, the King allowed people on this continent to decide some of these things, but when it came to taxation, he made the call. So that you understand, the reason the King suddenly enforced high taxes on the colonists is because England had been caught up in many wars, wars that had drained their coffers. So, he raised the taxes on goods going to and from America to help offset some of the costs of the wars as their economy was in deep trouble.

The colonial people in America found that they were working more than half the day just to pay money to the king. In some ways that was especially offensive, because if you understand the primary reason for migration from England to America, was because those people, our founding fathers, they wanted to get *out* of a repressive government like the one in England. They came here to be free.

When the taxation started, they realized that they had no say about it. So the people of that day, in this country, said enough is enough.

Let me remind you, in that day not everyone in America decided to go to war to get out from under the control of the King of England. The number got even less when it came to having to outfit yourself and soldier up and fight for your freedom. The war didn't look so good. But eventually, because of the American people and their desire to live free and their dedication to fight for it, allowed them to eventually win the war, with God's help.

When they won the war, they were thrust into a situation where they had to have some form of government. And no one knew what form of government we needed. The only thing everyone knew was that they're not going to be under the control of a king, to get rid of one king to just get another one. So, they set out to come up with a government that would work for them and all future Americans.

In that day, in the mid to late 1700's, there was a man named Alexander Tytler. He wrote about democracies and he studied them all the way back through history[1]. His conclusion was that they never worked. Because eventually, in a democracy, all we need do is get enough people to vote our way and when it's our turn at the trough, we'll have control. Never worked. A true democracy doesn't even work today. I don't I think I need to ask you when was the last time you heard a political person, a congressman or senator, say that we are a *representative republic*? Not knowing who you are, I'll bet that you haven't heard it hardly ever any more. They always refer to our form of government as a democracy.

Years passed, a lot of things happened - Civil War, War of 1812, WWI. The major changes affecting us today actually started to come about after WWII, over seventy years ago.

WWII. Let me give you a brief summary of that war and America during that time. WWII all but destroyed England, France, Germany, and Japan. All over the world countries were in ruins, even those areas of the world that won the war were in ruins from constant shelling. When the war ended, America was really the only country left standing, none of our factories were blown up. So, our soldiers came back home and went to work. Oh did we have a booming economy. Back then, the economy was that anything Europe and the other countries wanted, they weren't manufacturing, so they had to buy it from us. Millions and millions of Americans working. Then you had the model family. They would work, they'd build a nice little home, then retire. That was life's plan back then.

Eventually, that economy, that was all ours, our productivity, everything we did, we were the only ones doing it. But eventually, year in year out, some of these other countries were getting their infrastructures built back up, and started to come back alive, then they didn't need us as bad. So, this goes on and on for years.

Then, comes Bill Clinton. When Bill Clinton became

president, several things happened. Number one, the false economy that we were living in. I say it was false because those days of us making everything for everyone was gone, so jobs left.

Then, in came the computer. Oh my, what a revelation, what a world-changing instrument. That computer started running equipment in factories and they were laying more and more people off year over year. Bill Clinton saw our economy in trouble. So, he decided to create his own false economy to make everyone happy again. How did he do that? Well, since the world was turning everything over to the computer, Bill said, "Don't blame me, the computer did it. You need to retrain yourselves on the computer so that you can fit into today's new economy." The problem was that people didn't have the money to buy these new computer things. So, Bill worked out a plan with the key financial experts and banking institutions. Many of you will remember that he said, "I've got the ticket, we need to give credit cards to everyone so they can buy these computers, and since they've lost their jobs, we can use the credit cards to fund them until they get the new job." That was the plan. The outcome was a little bit different. You see, Bill Clinton built a false economy. That false economy went like this: the majority of households in America had about a $5000 debt through their credit cards when Bill Clinton took office. When he left office, the average family was $54,000 in debt!

Then comes George W. Bush. Now he's facing a dilemma. Bill Clinton's false economy was collapsing. People had borrowed all they could borrow. So, George Bush comes in and he builds *his* false economy. He did this through real estate. I'm sure many of you remember this period of time, there were ads on television that you saw every day, over and over saying refinance your home, and take that cash and pay off all those bills. Take that cash and go on vacation. And people did. And then, Bill Clinton's people had all of these laws changed to where people who couldn't afford to buy a home, could now buy a home, knowing full well that they couldn't pay for it, but they could still buy it! What did that serve you might ask? I'll tell you what it served. It made Bill Clinton look like a hero, because everyone could buy a home. But, eventually that would collapse. I believe it was in 2008 that it actually collapsed – that housing bubble burst.

So, what's our economy now? Ask yourself, what is our economy now? I see thousands and thousands of kids graduating college running up some of the biggest college debts in the history of our nation. I see them graduate with the degree in the field they want to be in. Then, I turn around and they're waiting tables in a restaurant. Why are they waiting tables? Because a new problem started coming up in America.

We were getting more and more lax about illegals coming in through our southern border from Mexico. Nobody cared. They'd say, "I live in *wherever* and I don't see any of them here, so it don't bother me." Nobody paid attention. I know, I grew up in a small town on the East Coast in the 1950's, 60's, and 70's and when I ventured out to California in 1972, I'd *never* seen a Mexican before, or even someone from the Middle East. But, now, Mexicans (not Mexican-Americans) live in my small town and nearly every other small town in America. More and more Middle Eastern people are taking over our neighborhoods in small town America, and we're just beginning to see court cases where certain Middle Eastern communities want to enforce Sharia Law[3,4]! Sharia Law is the antithesis of our Constitution and our American way of life.

Now when I said, not Mexican-Americans, here is what I believe. I am offended by these politically correct terms, Mexican-

America (term began in the 1950's), African-American (popularized by the film *Roots* and Jesse Jackson in the 1980's). We are Americans! No matter the skin color, no matter our country of origin, if we are here legally, whether we are natural born or naturalized citizens, we are Americans first! When the *powers that be* began breaking us up into separate groups, that's when the trouble began. Ever heard of *divide and conquer*? Well, that's their plan. To divide us up into groups, incite the groups against one another, then we will be easier to control and have less power over this *ruling class* that we've allowed to rule over us in America. Remember, *united* we stand, *divided* we fall. And fall we will if their plan continues.

Who are the *powers that be* and *the ruling class* you might ask? It's those that rule over us whether we realize it or not. It's those on that island in Washington D.C. and the lobbyists and rich elite that support them. It's the mainstream media (ABC, NBC, MSNBC, CBS, CNN, PBS, the major newspapers like the New York Times, Los Angeles Times, and Washington Post). It's the majority of those in Hollywood that make films meant to change our history and sway our traditional way of thinking. The *powers that be* and *the ruling class* purposefully sway us away from those American traditions that have made our country prosperous and a beacon of hope to all the world.

As much as I'd love to blame Bill Clinton (one of the many elite) for all the sins of the world that I can, and those illegals coming into this country, taking what few jobs are left, I must lay most of that blame right square on all of our backs. We *all* were lazy. You're always lazy until it affects *you*. Then, when it affects you, oh my gosh, it's the greatest problem on earth. But, by that time it's too late. So yes, our country changed drastically under Bill Clinton's rule.

Then in 2008 comes Barack Hussein Obama. He creates a world of problems, separating us further from our founding fathers and the principles by which our nation was founded. He separated us into groups to the greatest extreme ever! Many thought that when he became president, he was so brilliant, and that finally race might not be a factor in America anymore; when in fact, race had settled down, and it wasn't that big of a factor everywhere yet. It probably was in some major cities, but not in "middle of America nowhere town". But when Obama came in, racism started all over again.

And then, the Mexicans started coming in more and more because Obama opened up our borders and ignored the immigration laws designed to protect us from foreign invaders, who bring criminals and diseases, and people started noticing it. Factories were laying off Americans and hiring these illegals, and nobody cared. People scratched their heads, they couldn't figure out why their country was not taking care of them. Why did I lose my job to someone that's not even legal to be here? The reason is, the paradigm had shifted and the world had changed. Instead of all these illegals coming into the country and being a problem, politicians looked at them and said "that's a good thing". To Democrats that meant a lot of new people who could vote for them; Republicans saw them as a lot of cheap labor.

Well, baby would you look at us now in 2016! What a mess.

Those politicians in Washington D.C., they were on the take and I many of us knew it. But, most people couldn't see it. They were too busy living their lives and trusting those we elected to do the right thing for us. Now, I believe a lot of people in America are awake. At least many are awake. Finally, it came to the point to where *we* realized that *we* are affected by this. Remember what I said earlier? As long as we had our jobs, and everything was all hunky-dory, guess what? Life was good. But, then when it happened to us, oh it's the greatest problem on earth!

We, the American people are a pitiful, pitiful image of the people our forefathers and soldiers throughout all the wars fought to protect. Yes, a pitiful image of what they fought for and died for, and what they expected us to be.

Well, then the inevitable came. Hillary Rodham Clinton – it

was her turn to take over! Not just America, but her and Bill would finally be in a position to take over the world! I don't need to tell most of you how that campaign came out.

We now have president Donald Trump! The thing this election proved, at least to me, is that a lot of Americans were in deep trouble and they realized that we were suffering awful bad to be the greatest nation on earth. Then all of a sudden, they see this man running for president that just told the truth as he saw it and most of us saw it and promised to get it back. He promised to make us great again. Let me tell you, that promise will be hard for that man, Donald Trump, to keep. But, that's for another chapter.

So, this is where we are today (January 2017). So, when we ask the question, "How did we get to where we are today?" The answer is, we did it to ourselves. We did it! We didn't get out and work to make politicians do what we hired them to do. Somehow during this seventy-year period, going back to WWII, somehow things got twisted around, and those people in Washington, the congressmen, the senators, and the president, and all those secretaries of everything, things got changed. Instead of them working for us, they just told us we work for them. And when we would bring something out that we wanted, we'd go to our congressmen and senators, but they didn't hear us. Why can't they hear us? We're shouting. They don't hear us because we don't have money to give to them.

When George W Bush took office, there was some 1,800 lobbyists registered in Washington D.C. When he left, there was some 50,000! Ladies and gentlemen, it's those lobbyists that have the pull with the congressmen and senators – we don't. No, how we got to where we are today, has got to squarely be laid right on our shoulders, because we let it happen. That brings me to the next chapter, *What are we gonna do about it?*

CHAPTER 3. WHAT ARE WE GONNA DO ABOUT IT?

The answer is quite simple – war! To begin with, in this chapter, I want to make it perfectly clear, that I am a *nobody*. There is no particular reason why I should have or claim any credit to knowledge beyond that of anyone else in the country. But, I do ask this. Simply judge the things I tell you in this chapter on their own merit, not on mine. You see, far too long the people of this country have let others do their thinking for them. That time has come to an end. Now it's up to each and every one of us to form our own opinions and ideas about things that involve our families, our communities, and our country.

To begin with, when I say *war*, there will be two, or should I say a war on two fronts. One is external the other is internal. I'm not trying to position one above the other, but I will start with external.

Our enemies externally are two-fold, communism and Islam. Notice I said Islam, not *radical Islam*, because I believe Islam is an enemy to Christians all over the world, the two cannot coexist. They are a dichotomy.

Did you know that the Qur'an (their Bible) condones lying to non-Muslims? That's us! Yes, check it out yourself in the Qur'an. There are several verses in the Qur'an that are said to support lying. The most common is 2:26, taken from the Yusof Ali translation. Others include 2:225 and 16:106. In 2:26, it says, "The believers never ally themselves with the disbelievers, instead of the believers. Whoever does this is exiled from GOD. Exempted are those who are forced to do this to avoid persecution. GOD alerts you that you shall reverence Him alone. To GOD is the ultimate destiny."

So, a *true* Muslim must follow what their Qur'an says. If they do, then how can we trust them? Even those that claim to be our friend, who claim to be *peaceful* or *moderate,* or even worse – claim to be a Christian! Their Qur'an *commands* that they are *not* allowed to be friends with non-Muslims. In fact, it's been proven many times that they use the Christians' trust and naivety to manipulate them and take them over. So, as you can see, Islam in the antithesis of American values: truth, honor, respect, loyalty, freedom, individuality, patriotism, respect for others, and rule of law.

Communism breaks down into major components, one Russia and the other China. The wars between Russia and China and us will be different than wars before in history, due to the fact that all three of us are considered major powers, and have vast arsenals of nuclear weapons. Direct confrontation with any of us could lead to absolute mutual destruction, probably of the world. Therefore, our battle and struggle with communism will be dealt with through surrogates. So, the new world that we will be facing in the immediate future, will be that of lesser countries, lesser movements, backed by Russia and/or China, vs countries or lesser movements, backed by the United States of America. I have no doubt that the war I'm talking about is serious and more important - *inevitable*.

Russia will be our first opponent militarily. We can expect Russia to meet us on many different fronts with many different surrogates. China, however, will meet us in different ways. Number one, they have surrogates like North Korea. They have surrogates all over the globe, countries that depend on China or resources and money, but they also have another battlefront that is extremely dangerous to the United States of America, and that is the economy. You see, China has amassed vast holdings in American bonds, which they could throw into the marketplace at any time. By flooding the market with U.S. bonds, it would literally devastate our entire economic system in the United States of America. They also have captured much of the trade to the United States. Over the past years, China has captured many industries, once held as the bedrock of America, that are now gone. We are dependent on China for many, many products. So, therefore, at any moment, if China gets perturbed, they can shut down vital resources we need, and they can certainly stifle our economy by products that no longer can hit the shelves. It would take America years to recreate the industries that they now control. They also have the ability of playing with currency. You see, they can devalue their currency, and once again, with our economy in total shambles, put the dollar basically out of business.

So, what do you do with economic combat with China? One of the things that we can no longer do, is to no longer give in. See, China has a different philosophy with war than our country. We don't want war, but when we get in a war, we want to get in, fight it, win it, and get it over. Not so with China. China plans war over a hundred years. They steadily move in one direction, never rushing, never getting forced into a hurry, and their deliberate nature makes them incredibly formidable. And, they learned, not so many years ago, by another country named Japan, that the way to control the United States of America, was not with bullets and bombs, but with money. So, they started effectively buying our politicians in Washington. And today, I dare say, although it's not directly findable, but still, China probably backs more candidates running for Congress and the Senate than anyone else in the world. Believe me, those members that receive the benefit of this indirect financing know exactly where it comes from.

Over the years, we have been so void of leadership that believed in America, that we've gotten ourselves in a hole so deep, that it may not be possible to come out, short of a miracle. And far too long our Politians have one thing that they've cared about, and one thing only, and that was their career, their jobs, not that of the American people. China knew this and they used it, and they have used it on us, and they're using it today. There is a chance through new leadership that we may get a new type of leadership that provides an American first strategy and give us the basis for starting over, rebuilding; however, it will have to be done with a long-term strategy. American forces have been used all over the world to help train and lead surrogate countries to fight against the surrogates for China and Russia. That's our future, unless we change it.

Now for those of you that believe in fairy tales, look out, because you're going be in trouble. If you're not careful, you're going to put this nation under forever. So, stand strong.

Think about the things I've said. Read for yourself the news, the truth that can be told by anyone, certainly not by the mainstream media, that which you are to think. Don't be told by a Politian that which you are to believe. Decide for yourself and stand by that decision, and spread the word to people around you. Remember as I said earlier. The days of people in this nation to allow someone else to do their thinking, the planning, those days are gone.

That's what has us in this situation where the war is inevitable.

Next, we have the internal war. This one is very dangerous. You'll notice when I talked about the two enemies, I mentioned communism and Islam. When I told you about the external war, I mentioned Russia and China. I did not mention Islam, and you may wonder why. Was that just an error on my part? Did I just make a mistake? No, I didn't. You see, Islam is better categorized, although it is an external enemy, its better located in our internal wars. In the future, and I mean not distant future, you're gonna see internal strife within this country, like none we've seen before. Certainly, nothing we've seen in recent history. Organizations like Black Lives Matter, are going to start coming out front, taking their place in the country as a group, standing for anarchy, trying to bring any form of conservative moral Christian government at any level, to its knees.

Then, you have the liberals, the extreme liberals, who intend to push their agenda on this nation come hell or high water, they intend to destroy anything that has to do with Christianity, anything that has to do with leadership that might go against the liberal leanings of the Democratic Party. War will be imminent there.

Then there's the immigration problem. Immigration is going to provide two of the greatest armies that are inside our borders in the history of our nation. For the first time in America, a great war is going to happen right here in our land. Our buildings, our society is going to be blown apart, very similar to that in WWII. Oh yes, it's going to be that violent. You see, you have people from other countries that are pouring in here. They're not pouring in here to be part of the American experience. They're pouring in here to rape and plunder our economy to better themselves. They claim they're coming to run away from oppression and extreme hardship in the countries they come from. All at the same time, they come here and try to force on us their way of life.

They typically move into a small rural town, keep to themselves, keep the peace, and slowly grow in numbers quickly because in their belief system, they have multiple wives. In fact, the Qur'an allows and encourages men to have up to four wives! As they grow in numbers in their local communities, next thing you know they build a mosque, then they begin to take over the American way of life by slowing changing the local government to their form of government.

Never in the history, throughout all of history, have two opposing societies ever existed within one country and survived.

So, we have the Mexican invasion. By Mexican, I mean Latin America, the Latinos coming up through our southern border, taking over communities, taking over our streets, taking over our schools. Eventually, more and more they will be taking over our local and community governments.

We also have the rise of our greatest enemy of all - Islam. It is trapped, it has to grow to be able to exist. Islam, since the beginning of time, has made it very clear that it has two enemies. One, Israel and the other, anyone who supports Israel, like the United States of America. But they're not going to fight us externally. They're not going to take us on in the Middle

East. I hope and pray that American leadership, never again makes the mistake of thinking that we can go into the Middle East and force our way of life on them. They don't want it. They understand what we seem to not be able to grasp. That is, that Islam and Christianity or Judaism, they just don't mix. They don't mix at all. They can't coexist. They know it can't coexist. So, whenever we go in, we might win battles, and we might win battles over and over due to superior weaponry, training, etc., but we will *never* win a war there. Finally, I believe that the American people can figure that out.

Islam knows where the battle will be fought. It will be fought here inside our borders, in our land, in our country. Far too long we've had a policy of letting radical Islamists come in mixed in with so-called peaceful Islamists. Knowing of course that there's no way of knowing which one is or is not radicalized. Knowing also, that every day we allow radical

Islamists to infiltrate into our society, we run the risk of them spreading and growing more radical from within, better known as home grown terrorists. Soon, Islam will start taking its revenge on America.

Our leadership, weak as it has been, had better wake up, or it's all going to end. You see, our leadership uses our moral Christian conservative good people who believe that in trying to share and be nice will always try to compromise. But one day, in the not so distant future, in the interest of compromise, we're going to start allowing Islam to set up Sharia Law. It's only fair, they will say, since they represent such a big part of our community. But, folks when that happens, we will start the end of our nation as we've known it, and we'll start the beginning of the end of the world. Because this will become the battle between Christianity and Islam. I know it will eventually move over, as the Bible predicts, to the Middle East. But, it will start right here.

So, I tell anyone who reads this, that the thing you should be afraid of, is that you should know that war is imminent. We don't need, today, to be sitting back like we did in 1941 and be attacked totally by surprise by the Japanese on December 7th Pearl Harbor. There weren't any warning signs, just like today, for those who wanted to see them, but we chose not to see. We don't want that to happen again, because this time when that attack happens, it's going to be our country that's hit, and it's going to be our children, it's going to be our grandchildren, it's going to be our land that is thrust into a war that has no end. Because once you break this country, there will be no putting it back together again.

So, with that I tell you, the future is war, but there is one way out, and that's if every one of you will realize who we are, where we came from, take pride in being an America, take pride is being who we are, honor our heritage, and trust God to lead us. Don't let some other group push us aside. Stand strong, and if you do, and if you see wrong, correct it. Don't sit back and say that's somebody else's problem. We can save this country from war, but it's going to take each and every one of you who read this to do your part. Be active, be diligent, and win.

President Trump *can't* drain the swamp without your help!

CHAPTER 4. *ONLY WAY* TO SAVE AMERICA!

End the war! The only way to save our country is to end the war!

When Donald Trump was running for president, one of his campaign pledges was that he would *drain the swamp*! By that he meant that he would end the selling power and the absolute corruption running rampant in Washington D.C. The problem with this pledge is that he can't do it!

No president, or any one man can go to Washington and get the congressmen and senators to give up on their own what they've fought so hard to obtain and keep all these years. So, there is no way that Donald Trump or anyone else is going to *drain the swamp*. That does not mean that the swamp can't be drained.

Before I tell you how, there's one thing I need to clarify. You can never have a war if you don't know you're in a war. And once you acknowledge you're in a war, you can't win a war unless you can define victory.

So, let's be clear, we the people of the United States of America, are indeed in a war. No, it's not yet against Islam, at least not yet directly. It's not against the mean ol' Russians, not yet directly. The war we're in the middle of is a war against Washington D.C.

As I've stated earlier, is it now a war for the heart of our country, set up for an elite class, a class that plans to rule over all over of us, the peasants and peons. For far too many years, we the people of this country have sat back and allowed it to happen. Yes, *we* have allowed it to happen.

You see, we've adopted over the years a policy – well, let's elect this person or that person, and they will go to Washington and they will represent us, and our job is done. As most of you by now should know, that hasn't worked. Not only has it not worked, it never will work. So, what is the way to win a declared war against Washington D.C.? Is it a revolution? Is it a coup? Does there need to be blood in the streets?

All that needs to happen is for we the people to accept our responsibility that was given to us years ago by our founding fathers. You see, they knew that this day would come. They knew that from the day our country was established that there would be people trying to gain control and become the leaders and gather all the power unto themselves. They knew what that was like because they had just fought a war, a real war with blood in the streets and in the fields. With loss of life, of loved ones, families, and property. The reason they fought was because there was a king in another land far away who dictated what would be done here and how. And that king placed burdens on the people in this nation. Burdens so heavy, that they couldn't be carried by the average person. After all, the people of America had left that king's land for freedom, only to have it follow them here. We had a Revolutionary War and we won. But then our founding fathers did something that was *incredible* with God's help. They set out to design and construct a new form of government. A new form of government that ensured that the people of this land would forever be free of tyrannical governments, tyrannical leaders, and make sure that the people themselves ruled and that there would never be an island here. They gave us the Constitution. But, what was magical about our Constitution was the fact that they admitted they knew nothing about what they wanted to create, they had no idea, but they did trust God – after all, even our money states "In God We Trust". Oh, they had lessons from the past. They knew they didn't want a dictatorship, they knew they didn't want an oligarchy, they knew they didn't want a *democracy*.

So, the Constitution they drew up was one that was a *great experiment*. They didn't know *what* was best, but they had certainly lived through what was wrong.

Included in the Constitution were many things. We all know about freedom of speech, we know about the majority of the big items. But, there's one amendment to the constitution that over the years has fallen to the wayside, that was the Tenth Amendment – *states' rights*!

They included states' rights for one reason and one reason only. It was the intent of this new experimental government to see that it was run from the bottom up, never to be controlled from the top down. Do any of you understand what that means? Have you ever thought about it? They meant that the average every day person, living, struggling, raising his or her family, doing what they could to survive, that they controlled their destiny, not any one person or group. They put strict limitations on the Federal government. That was the great experiment. Could people rule themselves? Could people take charge of their own destiny? Could people truly govern themselves? At the close of the Constitutional Convention in 1789, Benjamin Franklin was quoted as saying to Dr. James McHenry, one of Maryland's delegates to the Convention, "Well, Doctor, what have we got—a Republic or a Monarchy? A Republic, if you can keep it." We've kept it for 227 years, but for how much longer? That's why it was called *the great experiment.* No one has ever done it before. No one knew if it could actually work. For over 200 years it worked in this nation. And then some tens of years ago, we started backsliding, and consequently we ended up where we are today. We have seceded powers both individually and at the state level to this island, this Washington D.C. This central government, which is really nothing more than kings and queens, and dukes and earls - just given other names, then we sat back and watched it happen. We've let it go. We've said well, it'll get better, it'll get better, and get better. But it didn't. It got worse, worse, and even more worse, until we found ourselves in 2016. We were at a turning point in this land. In the election of 2016, the American people, the average person finally was awoken, and realized, something's not right. And I think a lot happened just like with our founding fathers, a lot of people didn't know necessarily what wasn't right, and they certainly didn't know what was wrong, but they just knew *something's* not right.

Then, along came a man, a man named Donald Trump. He came shooting from the hip, he came telling things pretty flat out the way they were. In this election in 2016, many of the systems that had been in place to deceive the American people were exposed. People found out that the two-party system was actually one party, divided up so that people thought they had a choice. When in fact, it was all rigged and he said so, and many people listened. He also, for the first time, came out and openly attacked the media because they had been lying. They had literally been deceiving the American people. When people started to stand up and tell the truth, along would come this media, controlled by that central government in that island, which was Washington D.C. They would come along and smother that voice. He exposed it, people saw it. They saw that the media used polls that heretofore people thought were true representations of the people's feelings, they learned they weren't. He told the truth about many of the people in office in Washington D.C. and the person he was running against that was trying to get there. It was the dirty truth, but it was the truth nonetheless. People finally decided, yes, it's time to stand up, and they voted, and Donald Trump won!

So, what does all this have to do with *draining the swamp*? It goes back to what I said, he can't do it. Oh, he said he would do it, but he can't. Let me give you a simple example of why he can't do that.

Number one, to drain the swamp, he would have to put term limits on the members of the Congress and the Senate. To do that, you've got to get the members of Congress and the Senate to vote to limit themselves to a couple terms, rather than a life-long career, as a Politian living off the labors of the people of this nation. They would never do that. They won't do it, they never have, so it can't happen.

So, how do you *drain the swamp*? You go back to our founding fathers, they gave it to us, they gave us the answer, the Tenth Amendment. We were never supposed to be held hostage by a group of people in Washington D.C. that had all the power and we could not *touch* them, except once every two years or once every four or six years, come election time. It wasn't meant to be that way. The state was supposed to have the power. Each state was supposed to be sovereign, able to do for itself what its people needed. You have state governments, you have state legislatures, and you have governors. But, you see where we've come to today, doesn't come anywhere close to resembling what our founding fathers laid out for us. I guess the simplest and most brief explanation of this, is throughout the past few years, many states have tried to introduce laws that they wanted for their people, voted for by the people, ratified by their legislatures, signed by the governor, all within the law of the constitution of the state, only to find out that once passed, before it could be enforced, it would always be thrust into Federal court. Let's not forget that the Federal court is what? An extension of that island in Washington D.C. So, it goes to a Federal court, and some Federal judge with the stroke of a pen, stops the state from what it had duly and rightfully passed. To show you how wrong this is, it's very simple. Right now, would anyone believe we need governors, why now would anyone believe we need state legislatures? Because if this new way of doing business is the final way, we need only to do one thing. Find out what Federal court and what Federal judge has jurisdiction over the state, and whatever is requested, just go to that judge and say, "*May* we do it?" and the judge will tell you yes or no. Don't pay governors, don't pay legislatures, don't go to the trouble to have elections, don't do all of that, just go to the Federal judge, and that judge will dictate what you can or can't do. Now does that in any way sound like the America that you thought we lived in? Does it? Well, that's what we've got. And we got there through a thing called secession.

Throughout the years, states having Federal matching funds

waved at them, states have bowed down and seceded powers justly, rightly, dutifully bound to the state, over to the Federal government. It started out slow, but now it's manifested its way into every aspect of life. We now suffer at all levels: education, transportation, incomes, jobs, everything is controlled, not by the state, not by the people, but by the people that control that central government in that island known as Washington D.C.

So, for once in our lives, let's take advantage of the movement that happened in 2016 that got Donald Trump elected. Let's use that movement to fully declare the war on Washington D.C. and to remove its central government form of power, let's take advantage of Donald Trump, who has promised in his campaign that he was for turning things back over to the states. Let's declare that war and let's bring back the power to the people. And by that, the states need to take back the power from Washington D.C. Take it back! And then what happens? You, each one of you, you have to stay attentive, you have to stay vigilant. And the whole point of sovereignty at the state level, and the whole point of having state legislators, is so that within walking distance of where you live, you can talk to your state legislator, talk to your Senator, you can let your feelings be known. You and your neighbors can get together and make sure that your local representative knows your feelings, and then he or she can go to the state capital and make those feelings known, then the state legislature can amass the feelings of all the people of the state, and pass laws that fit the demands of the people of the state. No longer would it be that you have to make a request of a United States Congressman or Senator that you can't even get in touch with. You see, once they get to that island, they don't come back. The only time you even get to see them is election time and then they lie and tell you everything they're going to do for you, and when they go back, knowing that they're not going do it and they know you can't touch them! You see, it used to be that our congressional representatives served the will of the people. Ask them today, and you know what they'll tell you? In truth, if they won't lie to you and it's not election time, I'll tell you what they're going to tell you. They're going to say, "The people elected me to come here and exercise *my* will." And their will is based off one thing folks, and that's them keeping their job. As long as they're a United States Senator, who love the perks and the lavish lifestyle, they want to keep their job. And to keep that job, they must have money. And guess what? There are people known as lobbyists who are willing and able to shell out the money, as long as they do what they're told. And so they do. And so today we have the best government money can buy, problem is, the people don't have the money to buy it. States' rights is the answer to clean up this mess.

Donald Trump pledged to turn things over to the states to decide. I ask every one of you to pledge to make your governors and make your state legislators stand up and say, "This is ours and Washington you can't have it!" Demand that Donald Trump support the state in reclaiming its power. Never again back away from your job. Your job is to make sure that Donald Trump does what he says. Then, make sure your state representatives hear you, make sure your government hears you and let me tell you how fast we can turn this nation around. We don't have to wait through five or six cycles of changing out people in Washington. Even if it could happen, you're talking years and years before it could *ever* come together. We will be gone as a nation long before that could ever occur. One governor, one state, one state legislature, one people of a state, and one issue, standing up to the Federal government and to

Federal courts and saying "No!" When that day comes, when and if that day comes, this nation will be free again! Because when one state stands up and proves that the emperor has no clothes, proves that when the state wants to do something that's within the purview of the state to do, and the Federal government tries to intercede, and the state says no, the Federal government is left with nothing it can do about it. Nothing! Except one thing, and that's to use the leverage of money, Federal matching funds, blackmailing the state to go along with the wishes of the central government. And in truth folks, you just need to convince your state legislature and you need to convince your governors. And, you know what? Tell the Federal government to keep its money. Keep your money.

Let's take education. Keep that Federal matching fund, because you know what? What that Federal matching money has bought is the total destruction of our education system. Our children cost more to educate and they end up less educated. Keep the money. And then, the states need to exercise their side of it. If the Federal government wants to withhold matching funds, then states need to keep their own money and not send it to the Federal government. And I assure you that in almost all cases, the states will come out better. It truly will. But, if you use your rights as an American, your rights as a citizen in your state, I've got news for you, they can't be bought from you with Federal matching funds, if you're not willing to sell.

You see, it's called states' rights. Do you understand this is your *right*! Our founding fathers gave us this Tenth Amendment for this day to make sure that we would *never ever* get in a situation where some central power group or person rules the people of this land. But, in doing so, they left an awesome responsibility that's incumbent on each and every one of us to exercise our rights to make our feelings known, and to stand up for what we believe in. Stand up and make demands of the government because the government serves us, not the other way around.

So, the *war* is against Washington D.C. No, not a revolt where you take guns, not a coup where you go in with the military, no. The war is to stop it! Stop it from this illegal tyrannical ruling that has been going on far too long. And the victory is simple, give the power back to the people and to the states to where they reside.

Folks, if you do that, if we do that, in no time at all, America will look like a whole different country all over again. It will. There will be places that people can go that one state choses to do this, another state chooses to not do it, then the people of this country have a right to pick which one they want to go to. A state that believes and operates in the way you want it to be, and you can leave a state that doesn't. That's the way it's supposed to be. But, we the people must ensure that that's the country we live in now.

So, with that this book is complete. You may not think it is. You may have wanted some kind of long detailed analysis but there isn't any. Stand up and be counted, make your governors stand up and be counted. Make your legislatures stand up and be counted. Make sure your state legislators and local officials know who you are. And you make sure that you pay attention to what's going on around you, as well as in the world, and don't let anyone, and I mean anyone, ever get back in control of what you think. The cultural elite have proven they were wrong. They were not quite as elite as they thought. Stand up for what's right, stand up for your families, stand up for where you live, and trust God to do the rest. And if you do that, America will be free, I promise you.

May God Bless America!

References

[1]https://en.wikipedia.org/wiki/Alexander_Fra
ser_Tytler,_Lord_Woodhouselee

[2]https://en.wikipedia.org/wiki/The
Bible_and_slavery

[3]https://simple.wikipedia.org/wiki/Sharia law

[4]http://www.billionbibles.org/sharia/america-
sharia-law.html